CHESTER V

TEXT, GRAPHICS AND PUBLICATION BY

GORDON EMERY
27 GLADSTONE ROAD, CHESTER CH1 4BZ
www.gordomemery.co.uk

The Northgate by Jay Hurst

CONTENTS

CHESTER WALLS

The original walls at Chester were made of turf built in about 75AD by the Roman II Legion at their fortress DEVA. In around 102AD the XX Legion rebuilt the fortress walls in stone. The best remaining section of Roman wall under No1 City Walls can best be seen as a slightly bulging 13 courses of sandstone masonry looking east and upwards from the Northgate Bridge.

Centurial Stone: '(Built by) the century of Ocratius Maximus, in the first cohort' LMP may be reference to a thousand units of distance or the initials of the stonemason.

The walls were repaired again by the XX Legion a century or so later. The soldiers used old gravestones in its reconstruction. Up to 150 inscriptions, tombstones and sculptures were found built into the North Wall during the 19th century. Many are displayed at the award-winning Graham Webster Gallery at the Grosvenor Museum. Originally, they were painted in bright colours and would have lined the roads leading to the fortress.

In the tenth century, under Anglo-Saxon rule, Alfred's daughter Queen Aethelfleda probably extended the north wall to the river in the west, and the west wall to the river in the south, creating a walled town or 'burh' with a protected area four times the size of the former Roman fort. The remaining Roman fort walls on the south and west were removed or left to collapse. In Saxon and Norman times the walls were repaired by 'murengers' sent by the manorial lords of Cheshire. Walls and gates were built alongside the river by 1120.

The walls were fortified again in the Civil War to protect King Charles I's supporters inside the city against the Parliamentary forces attacking. Chester was the last city to hold out for the king, its citizens suffering hardship and starvation before surrendering.

King Charles Tower

In Georgian times the walls became a fashionable walkway around the city, completed with the construction of the Wishing Steps in 1785. The main city gates were removed to allow access for coaches and were replaced by grand archways. In the 1830s, a section of wall was knocked down when an access road was built to the new Grosvenor Bridge. Another section was removed and bridged over for the railway in 1845. When Castle Drive was built alongside the river a short section of wall was removed and the old Shipgate was moved to Grosvenor Park, then, with the increased use of the motor car, an inner ring road was driven through the north wall in the 1960s. Today visitors can still walk around the unique and almost complete wall around the city.

WALK THE WALLS

The city can be circumnavigated by using the city walls. This guide splits it into four quarters. **Walk around the city walls from any main gateway to the next or follow the complete circuit 2km around the city.** On the way you will see ancient and modern gates and towers. Watch the life of the busy shopping centre from the Eastgate Clock, leave the walls to visit the Roman amphitheatre or take a boat trip on the River Dee. Visit the Castle, watch the horse races on the Roodee or be a 'gongoozler' watching narrowboats climb the staircase lock on the Chester Canal. Imagine King Charles watching the defeat of his army or take a look at the falcons on the Cathedral green.

Instructions for sloped access are given at the beginning of each quarter.

Eastgate to Northgate (Cathedral and Civil War)
Sloped access beside the belltower (St Werburgh Street). Return and exit from here or by Kaleyards Gate (leading to Frodsham Street). Steps over the Eastgate.

The ornamental clock on the Eastgate was built for Queen Victoria's Jubilee in 1897 but, like all public works, it took longer than expected and cost more money. Finally a local solicitor paid for the clock mechanism and it was erected in 1899, just in time for Victoria's 80th birthday. Until 1973, when electric winding was introduced, the firm of J B Joyce wound the clock each week. In 1992 the whole mechanism was replaced with an electric one. Before digital cameras, visitors used a tonne of paper each year just printing photos of this colourful highlight to the city.

The medieval gateway here, incorporating the Roman one, was too small for coaches and was demolished in 1768. In medieval times everyone entering with goods to sell had to pay a toll:

Of eney lode of salte entringe at the saide gate – a farthing
All soe of eny lode of coles entringe at the said gate – one colebronde
Allsoe for eny lode of eathen potte – one potte
Allsoe for eny lode entringe with woode to be solde – one bough nother a worse or a better
And for every horselode entringe with hay, one handeful

4

From the Eastgate, walk north (anticlockwise). Here the wall is on its original Roman course and the footings are Roman.

You soon reach the Cathedral, its freestanding belltower and Garden of Remembrance. Until 1341 this was the Abbey of St Werburgh. The west face of the Cathedral shows the extensive restoration carried out by Sir George Gilbert Scott who was entrusted with major Gothic Revival works of the time. William Morris, founder of the Society for the Protection of Ancient Buildings thought Scott destroyed many ancient buildings with little thought for their texture or substance.

The freestanding Addleshaw Tower, built in 1975, holds 13 of the cathedral bells.

The pattern in the garden represents a medal and ribbon in memory of the 22nd Cheshire Regiment soldiers who gave their lives in World War II.

To the right is Frodsham Street Car Park. Once used to grow hops for the abbey's brewery and cabbages for the monks, later the horse paddock for the Hop Pole Inn, it was saved from becoming the site of an electric power station and a swimming baths in the late 19th century through its purchase by the Dean and Chapter as a public open space. They, however, had not foreseen the growth of the automobile industry and might today be shocked by its current use.

Stop by the next slope. An anchor cut into the outer wall 692 feet from the south wall of King Charles Tower in the distance, by a master mason of Chester and the owner of a nearby timberyard, celebrates the launch of the Great Eastern steam paddleship with a length of 692 feet launched in 1858 by Isambard Kingdom Brunel. The double-hulled ship was four times the size of other ships of the period and made completely from iron. One wonders if these two gentlemen, like thousands of others, went to the launch or just read about it in the paper.

692ft anchor mark

Below you is the Kaleyards Gate. Originally built for the monks to attend to their vegetable gardens in the 13th century, it was used as a sally port to attack the enemy (Parliamentarians) in the Civil War during the mid-17th century. Every night it is still closed after ancient custom at 9pm by the Cathedral, a quarter hour after the single curfew bell, still in the Cathedral Tower, is tolled.

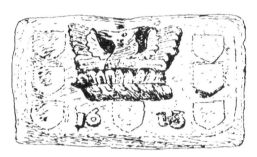
The phoenix on King Charles Tower

At the northeast corner of the wall stands the King Charles Tower. The phoenix carving is the emblem of the Painters, Glaziers, Embroiderers and Stationers Company, a city guild who held their meetings here and, in 1613, were given permission to repair the roof which was *uncouered with leade and rayne discending upon and into the same.*

However, during the Civil War, the guild met in safer Watergate Street while the tower was used for defence.

King Charles I watched from the top as his beaten Cavaliers pulled back from the Battle of Rowton Moor into the suburbs, then he took refuge in what he thought was the safer Cathedral Tower. He was proved wrong again when a musket ball killed the captain standing next to him. The king retreated to Wales leaving the city holding out until starvation took place the following year.

In 1854 a Mr Benjamin Huxley was allowed to rent the top floor at a rent of 2s6d a year provided that he *only use it as an observatory.*

Below, the Chester Canal was started in 1772. It is said that the contractors for the cut made a saving when, instead of having to cut the canal through solid rock, they only had to remove centuries of rubbish tipped over the walls since Roman times. Unfortunately the canal ended at Nantwich without joining the main network so that, only eight years later, shares in the canal company were worthless. It was only when the Ellesmere Canal Company joined it in 1795 that it began to flourish. The companies merged, and merged again into the Shropshire Union. On his stroll around the walls in 1872, American writer, Henry James, saw *burly watermen in smocks and breeches.*

In the Civil War turf ramparts were built to strengthen the city wall. Dead or injured bodies could quickly be removed with no rear wall on the parapet.

At the first building on your left is the entrance to Rufus Court and the steps down to Alexanders Beer Garden. This small shopping courtyard with its own jazz theatre won an award for its internal row design imitating the traditions of the medieval city. Take a quick look before continuing.

Opposite, carefully look over the wall ramparts to see the top course of the Roman wall below. This is the best section of the surviving Roman defence. From here can be seen the top of the carved cornice and rebated foundation stone to support the parapet wall. Below (view safely from the Northgate Bridge) are thirteen courses without mortar on a chamfered plinth.

To leave the walls here, go down the steps through Rufus Court, or the steps by the Northgate and turn left to the city centre. The only sloped exits are by returning to the Cathedral.

Northgate to Watergate (Canal and Old Port)

Unfortunately there is no wheelchair access from the Northgate to St Martin's Gate (the bridge across St Martin's Way). The only sloped access to the later section of wall is opposite the former Infirmary 1763 on City Walls Road where the wall is alongside the pavement.

The earlier Northgate on this site contained the remains of the Roman gateway in it and the city gaol beside it. On 30th May 1578 the whole company of city butchers were imprisoned here for not suppling enough meat to citizens while forming a confederacy against country butchers. To be incarcerated in the airless, dark cells was not a pleasant fate and they were released on the 13th June after their humble submission to the mayor.

The Bridge of Sighs
Prisoners condemned to die suffered the 'drop' at the gaol after they had crossed the narrow bridge from their last visit to the chapel in the Bluecoat Hospital.

From the Northgate walk westwards (anticlockwise) above the Liverpool Arms. The Bluecoat Hospital is built on a site outside the walls, formerly occupied by the medieval Hospital of St John the Baptist. Pensioners later housed here were given *a good loaf daily, a great dish of pottage, a piece of flesh or fish and half a gallon of competant ale.* There are still almshouses at the rear of the building, added when the hospital was enlarged in 1854. The building of 1717 incorporated the Bluecoat School, the first charity school built outside London by the Society for the Promotion of Christian Knowledge.

Further along, in the park below, are the rebuilt capping stones on the Roman Wall shown on the front cover.

You soon reach a square tower. Morgan's Mount is named after a captain in the Civil War who sited his cannon here. From this point, centuries earlier, the Roman wall would have turned southwards. You are about to follow the extension west built in the 10th century to fortify the Saxon burgh, which created the foremost medieval city in northwest England.

Below, on the canal, Northgate Locks were cut out of sandstone. Originally there were five leading down to the river but when the Wirral Arm of the Ellesmere Canal was cut from the corner below, a new course led down to the river through the lower basin.

Pass a half-round tower. Formerly the Goblin Tower, it was later named Pemberton's Parlour after a rope manufacturer (Pemberton) who watched his men working from the walls. Below in the little park is a tree sculpture by Martin Heron.

Telford's Warehouse, now a canalside pub, was named after Thomas Telford, General Agent, Surveyor, Architect and Overlooker of the Works on the canal. The original Ellesmere Canal Tavern was next door. Its proprietor did a brisk business running a fast packet boat from Liverpool from here in the 19th century. As well as food on the boat, the inn offered ...*good Beds, Wines, Spirituously malt liquors for the entertainment of families, Travellers & the public in general whose favors he humbly solicits assuring them it will be his constant study to merit their Approbation and support.*

The Dee Basin entrance to the canal (old engraving)

Below you the canal turns north as you reach two corner towers. The closer one, pockmarked with the damage from musket balls during the Civil War, is the strangely named Bonewaldesthorne's Tower. In medieval times the River Dee travelled through the arch crossing the span from the walls to the Water Tower - a port watch tower built in 1322. The boat-shaped building beyond the tower is a scout hut.

The River Dee was canalised in the18th century. The wharves for the port and the Harbourmaster's House lie beyond the modern buildings on its altered course. A guide of 1851 noted the scenery from here: *The beautiful view of the winding Dee and the picturesque country on its banks is most delightful and cannot fail to excite very pleasurable emotions.*

Chester Quay (old engraving)

The Water Tower Gardens hold one ancient artefact, a bluestone which may be the 'Glover's Stone', moved here from a noted boundary between the city limits and the township of Gloverstone which had, at its hub, the old Chester Castle with the shire headquarters. Criminals or vagabonds were handed over ...*att glovers stoune to such officer of the Cittie of Chester, in and from hence to whipp them through the Citie.*

The Chester & Holyhead Railway works began by felling trees here in 1845. However trains had already reached the city on another line. In 1840 the steam engine 'Wirrall' pulled 10 carriages into Chester Station.

In the distance is the Clwydian Range of North Wales hills with Moel Fammau prominent because of the ruined tower on its summit, originally a tall tower for George III's Jubilee built by Thomas Harrison. The Grosvenor Museum holds a medallion depicting the restoration of the tower for Queen Victoria's Jubilee nearly a century later, but due to lack of funds the monument was never rebuilt so only three of the medallions were cast.

Moel Famau medallion

Pass the Infirmary and the Queen's School on your left. The Infirmary, first opened in the Bluecoat Hospital in 1756 but moved here five years later, was one of the first hospitals to have isolation wards for infectious diseases. It was converted to luxury apartments, some complete with roof gardens, in 2001.

Terracotta fronts the Queen's School, opened in 1883. The house of Correction once stood on the site. Further along Sedan House could shelter the well-to-do occupants of sedan chairs as they entered the house. The chairmen had to put up with the weather at each end. Chester had as many as fifteen licensed carriers in the17th and 18th centuries who catered mainly for ladies with long dresses while the gentlemen, in boots, usually walked.

To leave the walls here turn up Watergate Street by the traffic lights to the city centre. *To avoid the steps over the Watergate you need to cross the road on the footway by the lights.*

Watergate to Bridgegate (Racecourse and Castle)

This section of the walls has no steps between the two gates, and is accessible for wheelchairs: access from Nuns Road.

Tolls from 1321 show some of the produce carried into the city from the river just outside the Watergate: *...of every horselode of mussells one little dishfull ...of every horselode of great fishe, a quarter of a fish or the heade or one penny.*

Nuns Road

Pass the racecourse entrance. England's oldest racecourse hosts 12 days of races a year. It was the brainchild of reformist Mayor Henry Gee who, in 1540 cancelled the traditional Shrove Tuesday game where *one ball of lether caulyd a fout boule to play from thens* (the Roodee) *to the comen hall* because it was becoming too violent. He replaced it *with a bell of sylver ... to whom shall run best and furthest upon horseback.*

His attempts to stop people playing football failed though. In 1564, *there was a great Frost, and the Dee was frozen over, so that people played football thereon.*

The first paying gate meeting at the racecourse was in 1893 when, despite the one shilling minimum charge, 50,000 people turned up in three days. In fact, crowd control was so difficult that the Chief Constable let in about 200 free to stop a woman being crushed at the turnstile.

Kings, queens, dukes and earls have regularly visited Chester Races ever since. Perhaps the surest and shortest odds were here in 1896 when Baron de Rothschild's horse, Amandier, romped home at 1/25 on.

Better turf, tents and viewing have been added over time. In 1985 the old County Stand burnt down and was replaced by the new larger red-tiled stand, also used as conference rooms and a restaurant 1539. (Shrove Tuesday in 1540 was then in 1539.)

The road on your left, Black Friars, lies on the boundary of the former friary.

White friar Grey friar Black friar
(Carmelite) (Franciscan) (Dominican)

Just beyond Black Friars, look over the curve of the city wall to the sandstone blocks of a wall known as the Roman Quay. It goes underground to a depth of five metres as far as the Watergate, and must have separated the river from the land and acted as an outer defensive wall. One of the Roman dockhands must have been a little careless: a lead ingot was found here in the mud.

Lead ingot at the Grosvenor Museum

The small stone pillar beyond the racetrack is the base of a cross that may have given this area its name: Roodee from rood (cross) and eye (island). Over time the river was moved to its present course leaving the racecourse fairly dry. The Roodee is a public open space except on race days. Feel free to go for a walk, a run, or fly a kite on the large treeless area. In the 16th century Mayor Gee ordered that boys should practice with the longbow here, their parents supplying the bows and arrows.

The Architect pub was built as the house of Thomas Harrison, mentioned later.

Nuns Road here was once just a green in front of the medieval St Mary's Nunnery. Later Nunnes Hall became the home of Sir William Brereton, the Cheshire MP who was 'persuaded' to leave the city in the Civil War. When he returned in triumph with the Parliamentary forces he found that the Royalist supporters had burnt his house to the ground.

Leave Nuns Road using the lights to cross the main road. To your left is the equestrian statue of Field Marshal Combermere GCB (1773-1865). He was born in Denbigh, served with Wellington and as Governor General in India, and was the Grand Master of Cheshire Freemasons. Most soldier's statues are placed with the hero riding into the city, but Combermere was not in the Cheshire Regiment so his horse is riding out!

The medieval Agricola Tower in the Castle was once thought to be Roman, thus its name.

Continue on the walls just above Castle Drive. The original castle mound is probably Norman; Henry II started rebuilding the original wooden structure with stone in 1245. Grosvenor Bridge with its single span stone arch was the longest in the world when it was opened by Princess Victoria in 1832 to the sound of a 21 gun salute. The bridge, to your right, the Propylaeum (castle entrance) designed in Greek Revivalist style and the modern castle to your left, were by Thomas Harrison. His other claim to fame is that he persuaded Lord Elgin to collect Greek antiquities. The Elgin Marbles were given to the British Museum and have caused controversy ever since.

Thomas Harrison's model bridge built to display the design before it was built, now situated below the wall on Castle Drive.

At the end of the wall turn left along the road to reach the Bridgegate and the old Dee Bridge. There was once another small gate on the river's edge known as the Shipgate. Its arch is now in the Grosvenor Park. On the far side of the Bridgegate was another gate, the Caple Gate or horsegate where horses could get to the river edge to drink.

Position of the Shipgate marked in the slope to the Bridgegate

Beside the bridge is the first hydro-electric station built in a city to power a city, with three turbines running in 1913 supplying a third of the city's requirements at that time, at a fifth of the cost of the coal-fired generators. It is on the site of the former Dee flour mills immortalised in the 'Miller of Dee' written by Bickerstaff in the 18th century, "I care for nobody, no not I, if nobody cares for me". The miller's song is based on the accusations that millers took more than their share of grain in payment.

The Old Dee Bridge

The Old Dee Bridge is near the site of the Roman bridge into the city. On the far side of the river, in the park, is a Roman statue of the goddess Minerva, who was probably set there to bless the safety of Romans crossing the river. This Roman idol survived destruction because people once thought it depicted the Virgin Mary but the owl on her shoulder should have given it away.

Turn left up Bridge Street to the city centre or continue along the next section of wall over the Bridgegate.

Detail on the Bridgegate

Bridgegate to Eastgate (River Dee and Amphitheatre)

Disabled access is severely limited on this section of the walls as each of the four ramps only serves a short section of wall. There is one at the Bridgegate, one from the junction of Park Street and Duke Street (steep), one by lift from Pepper Street Car Park, the other from the Grosvenor Precinct.

A more interesting route for wheelchairs or those who want to avoid steps can be found by continuing along the riverbank for 200 metres then turning left up through the Roman Gardens to the Newgate. Do not go through the gate but turn right to the amphitheatre and, using the pedestrian lights, first left up St John Street to the Eastgate.

The old Bridgegate had a large square tower built on its centre in 1600. This combined with pipes from upstream and a water wheel on the weir, pumped water into the city, the first such system outside London. In the Civil War the tower was destroyed. When Daniel Defoe visited the city in 1690, water had to be carried up the hill in leather vessels on horseback. However, in 1692, a new octagonal water tower was built on the west side of the gate. In 1731 the clerk of the works suffered a dreadful accident when he *stood upon a plank in the water engine to oyl the brasses there he accidentally slipped and fell down headlong under the crank ...he received a mortall wound or was crushed and bruised by the said crank that he instantly dyed.* Later, the waterworks were replaced upstream but the tower remained until the present arched gateway was built.

Tyrer's Tower 1600-45

Follow the wall eastwards (anticlockwise) past the remains of the round tower. Ignore the next steps on your right unless you want to go down to the riverside (the Groves). The steps are named after the city's top judge: the Recorder.

Go up the 'Wishing Steps'. If you can run up and down them whilst holding your breath your wish may come true. The original legend was only for young women looking for husbands but the tale has grown with the telling.

To your right are the Roman Gardens which can be accessed by going down the slope on your left then through the small gate under the wall. Displays of Roman columns stones and *pilae* from the Roman baths create a long park between the river and the Newgate.

To the left is the Albion pub, full of World War I memorabilia. Further on are the six remaining 'nine houses', former almshouses with their unusual solid base and timber-framed uppers. Above the car park is a lion statue from the former brewery on the site.

Unless you want to descend the steps to visit the amphitheatre, cross the modern Newgate. This gate was built to widen access in 1938. Next to it stands the former Newgate also known as the 'Peppergate' or 'Wolfgate', rebuilt in 1608. Its unusual name may come from the Norse personal name *Ulfaldi*, or from the carved wolf's head above the former gate, the wolf was a symbol on the coat of arms of Chester's first Norman earl, Hugh d'Avranches (Hugh Lupus).

The gate now leads to the ruin of the Southeast Angle Tower, originally inside the Roman fort: a collapse of the Roman wall led to the new line of the wall further back. From here the course of the southern Roman wall followed the present Pepper Street. The section of wall you have just walked was an Anglo-Saxon addition to enlarge the fortified city.

The Wolfgate, also known as the Peppergate or Newgate rebuilt in 1609

Just beyond a tower is the entrance to the Grosvenor Precinct. Partially destroyed in the Civil War, Thimbleby's Tower now has a mock-medieval roof.

Steps on your left head down to Eastgate Street and Foregate Street. If you want to continue around the walls go to page 4.

The Eastgate Clock

CHRONICLE OF CHESTER WALLS

AD/CE c50s/60s A small primary Roman fort may have existed at Chester.

c74 Roman fortress walls made from timber with turf ramparts and ditch by II Legion.

c102   Roman stone walls started by XX Legion.

c163 Wall building renewed as XX Legion returns from Hadrian's Wall.

c383 Magnus Maximus takes much of the legions abroad in a revolt against Rome. They never return but a garrison appears to have held Chester up to the 390's.

c417 Roman General and Bishop, St Germanus, deposes Vortigern (great King) the last Ruler of all Britain, accusing him and the British bishops of heresy. Chester or adjacent North Wales may have been the location for this, and at least one Bishop was based nearby. Thereafter the country deteriorates into petty tribalism, and Saxons begin to overrun (what is now) England.

c418 Anglo-Saxon Chronicle records that "*This year the Romans collected all the treasures that were in Britain, and some they hid in the earth…*"

c475 In legend, Arthur fights his ninth battle at 'the city of the legions' (may have been Chester or Caerleon).

c603 Synod of the British church held in Chester suggests that the city has become an ecclesiastical centre.

613 Battle of Chester: King Ethelfrith of Northumbria defeats the Welsh (British) and slays 2000 monks from Bangor-on-Dee.

c660 St Peter and St Paul's Church founded inside the walls on the site of the present Cathedral.

894 Alfred besieges Danes in Chester.

c693 Giraldus states that St John's Church is founded (outside the walls).

c912 Aethelflaeda creates a fortified burgh by the simple method of extending the north and east walls to the River Dee thus creating a fortified burgh (it is now believed that some of this extension may have been based on a similar Roman extension).

c1057 During an attack on the city by King Gruffydd (Gruffyddap-Llewellyn) the remains of St Werburgh were carried onto the walls and are said to have 'struck the king blind'. A stained glass window in the Cathedral commemorates this tale.

1086 The Domesday Book records that: for the repair of the city walls and bridge the reeve used to call up one man from each hide in the county. The lord of any man who failed to come was fined 40s shared between the king and earl.

c1120 Bridgegate and Shipgate built.

c1150 Western walls built, partly along Roman 'quay' wall.

1275 Monks build 'Kaleyards Gate' to reach their vegetable gardens.

1303 Wolfgate/Peppergate mentioned as 'Wofuldegate'.

1307 Murage duty taken to keep the walls in good repair.

1321 Tolls at the Watergate include: *'of every horselode of mussels one little dishful… of every horselode of great fishe, a quarter of a fishe or he headd or one penny'.*

1322   Port Watch Tower (now called the Water Tower) built to extend the walls to the new course of the River Dee for £100.

1499 Midsummer Watch Parade started, a colourful parade that linked the walls, the church, the civil authority and the people. There was also a Christmas Eve Watch: a candlelit procession would go from the Mayor's house to the Common Hall where the keys to the city gates would be given to the mayor who, in turn, entrusted them to the watchmen who would keep the city safe over Yuletide.

1569 The two city sheriffs were fined £10 towards repairing the walls.

1573 The Newgate /Peppergate/Wolfgate is locked after Mayor Aldersey's daughter elopes through it; later in the year it was just locked at night. This gave rise to a Chester saying "locking the Peppergate after the daughter had gone", similar to the saying about locking the stable door after the horse has bolted.

1589 Harre Tower on the medieval and Roman Eastgate rented to one of the city companies for an annual rent of 6d.

1599-1600 John Tyrer builds square tower in the centre of the Bridgegate as a water storage tower, pumping water up by a waterwheel on the Dee, and thence by pipe to the city.

1608/9 Wolfgate rebuilt.

1613 The companies of Barber Surgeons, Tallowchandlers and Wanchandlers together with the company of Painters, Glaziers Embroiderers and Stationers as tenants of the Phoenix Tower (now King Charles Tower) complained that it was *'uncoered with leade and rayne discending upon and into the same'* and petitioned the Assembly to let them repair it.

1620 more repairs on the Phoenix Tower.

1692/3 Phoenix (emblem of the Stationer's Company) carving by Randle Holme III put up on Phoenix Tower by Edward Nixon.

1640 Sep 18 City watch continued at night.

1642 Jan 1 (New Year started in March) Murengers request money to repair walls. Sep 6 100 marks assessed on citizens to repair walls.

1643 Nov 11 6 gates have 8 guards - 4 with muskets, 4 with halberds. Dec 1 Parliamentarian troops encircle city. Prince Maurice later relieves city.

1644 Chester siege resumed. King Charles later relieves city.

1645 The King, on the Phoenix Tower, watches his troops fight in the suburbs after losing the Battle of Rowton Moor. For safety he moves to the Cathedral Tower but even here his captain next to him is shot in the head.

Dec 30 After the King has fled, Brereton reports the complete encirclement of Chester. The city surrendered (after having refused 9 times) on Feb 3. Tyrer's water tower destroyed, Thimbleby's Tower (named after Lord, and Lady Thimbleby who died in Chester 1615) partially destroyed, breaches in the east wall.

1662 John Crewe released the right of tolls from the Eastgate to the Assembly in return for rent from the Roodeye.

1692 Hadley and Hopkins build octagonal water tower on west side of the Bridgegate to resupply the city with water.

1693 date with the initials RH (Randle Holme) carved into Kaleyards gate may have been the date of a rebuild.

1700 Recorder's steps built to the south wall.

1707 City Assembly made a grant of £1,000 to repair and re-flag the walls to make a walkway with an unfortified parapet. Morgan's Mount rebuilt.

1717 Bluecoat Hospital built outside Northgate.

1719 The unfortunately named Ann Edge falls from walls by Phoenix Tower.

1768 Eastgate pulled down, parts of Roman gate found. Aug 8th cornerstones of Eastgate arch laid by Aldermen, Mayor and sheriffs.

Thomas Boswell petitions to build steps to Abbey Green.

1769 Eastgate arch completed by Mr Hayden, funded by Richard Lord Grosvenor.

1778 April 5th A huntsman of the Chester Harriers, for a wager, rides around the walls, leaping two turnstiles, in 9½ minutes.

1772 Chester Canal started to be cut below walls. Workers find that the Roman ditch is full of rubbish.

1782 Bridgegate rebuilt as an arch by Joseph Turner.

1785 Wishing steps built.

1789 Turner builds new Watergate Arch.

1793 Turner builds 'Bridge of Sighs' to join Northgate Gaol to Bluecoat chapel for prisoners.

1808 Northgate Gaol demolished.Thomas Harrison builds Northgate arch commissioned by Robert, Second Earl Grosvenor.

1830 Morgan's Mount repaired.

1832 Grosvenor Road cuts through city walls to Grosvenor Bridge, the first new entrance to the city since medieval times.

1836 Tolls at city gates discontinued.

1838 Shipgate removed, now in Grosvenor Park)1854 Top floor of King Charles' Tower let as an observatory to Mr Benjamin Huxley for 2s6d per annum. Camera obscura mounted in Bonewaldesthorne's Tower by the Mechanics Institute.

1845-6 Chester and Holyhead Railway cut through northwestern corner of city walls and is bridged over.

1854 Copper rod and anchor carving with initials DS (District Surveyor) set in Bridgegate as a benchmark.

1858 An anchor with 692Ft carved 692 feet south of the southern wall of King Charles' Tower by Mr William Haswell, mason, and Mr Musgrave, timberyard owner, to celebrate the launch of the Great Eastern, an enormous iron ship built by Brunel originally called The Leviathan.

1879 Tramway opened through Eastgate going from Chester

Station to Saltney, these were converted to electric trams just over 20 years later.

1879 Watch Tower by Wishing Steps taken down.

1881 I Matthews Jones, the city surveyor, finds Roman gravestones in North Wall near Phoenix Tower. They are stored in the Water Tower Gardens where some disappeared and others eroded. They are then recognised as the best preserved set of gravestones in Northern Europe and are now displayed at the Grosvenor Museum in a special gallery.

1894 Goblin Tower (later known as Pemberton's Parlour) rebuilt.

1899 Eastgate Clock started at 12.45 on Queen Victoria's 80th birthday, two years after it was designed for her Jubilee.

1903 Buffalo Bill photographed with 'cowboys and Indians' by the walls in the Roodeye for his 'Wild West' show.

1938 New Newgate built in mock medieval style to allow widened Pepper Street traffic but the wrong way round as the arrow slits face inwards.

1966 St Martin's Gate, an arch over the inner ringroad, opened by transport minister Barbara Castle.

1975 Addlestone Tower built beside Walls to house most of Cathedral bells, except the curfew bell, still in the Cathedral.

1984 New camera obscura fitted in Bonewaldesthorne's Tower.

1995 Rufus Court built adjoining walls with internal 'rows'.

2012 After an extensive survey both minor and major repairs to the walls begin.

2013 A new viewing platform built when King Charles Tower restored.

2014 'Friends of the walls' established.

The District Surveyor's benchmark of 1854 under the arch
of the Bridgegate includes a set-in copper rod and a carved anchor

Printed by Catford Print Centre, London SE6 2PN   www.catfordprint.co.uk